SATURN PEACH
BY LILY WANG

Gordon Hill Press

Guelph, Ontario

Copyright © 2020 Lily Wang

All rights reserved. No part of this work may be reproduced or used in any form, except brief passages in reviews, without prior written permission of the publisher.

Edited by Shane Neilson
Cover and interior illustrations by Elijah White
Cover and book design by Jeremy Luke Hill
Proofreading by Carol Dilworth
Set in Garamond and Eraser
Printed on Mohawk Via Felt
Printed and bound by Arkay Design & Print

LIBRARY AND ARCHIVES CANADA CATALOGUING IN PUBLICATION

Title: Saturn peach / by Lily Wang.
Names: Wang, Lily, 1997- author.
Description: Poems.
Identifiers: Canadiana (print) 20200220977 | Canadiana (ebook) 20200220985
    | ISBN 9781774220115 (softcover) | ISBN 9781774220122 (PDF)
    | ISBN 9781774220139 (HTML)
Classification: LCC PS8645.A5324 S28 2020 | DDC C811/.6—dc23

Gordon Hill Press respectfully acknowledges the ancestral homelands of the Attawandaron, Anishinaabe, Haudenosaunee, and Metis Peoples, and recognizes that we are situated on Treaty 3 territory, the traditional territory of Mississaugas of the Credit First Nation.

Gordon Hill Press also recognizes and supports the diverse persons who make up its community, regardless of race, age, culture, ability, ethnicity, nationality, gender identity and expression, sexual orientation, marital status, religious affiliation, and socioeconomic status.

Gordon Hill Press
130 Dublin Street North
Guelph, Ontario, Canada
N1H 4N4
www.gordonhillpress.com

CONTENTS

PART 1 - RE: 1
PART 2 - UNSOLICITED PORTRAITS 17
PART 3 - ARCADE 27
PART 4 - BLUE OLIVES 45
PART 5 - CONCERT 65

I am rowing towards something yellow and frightening. I am rowing away from myself into myself. In a dream where I decide everything. I decide I am edible. I decide to eat a peach. Reflections on the snow. The water Saturn. Don't decide yet. Go round and round. In my memory it's always me.

PART 1

RE:

RE: NOTHING SPECIAL

When you say the past catches up to you—
when it shines like a sprite, offering sweets filled with sea brine—
when you say when (the past catches up):

I am already in the future.

The soles of my feet dangling above the water,
I am three times the weight of a song. Sea brine:
this is the only way it can happen (the past)
and I know you don't mean one (catching up).

I know you are not speaking of numbers at all;
it gets confusing; who drapes what on what, on who?
It gets confusing and we run out of fingers. We pass.

Isn't salt supposed to help with that? (the passing).

MAGIC HOUR CONFESSIONS

I love to make people cry. I love to make them smile. Sadistic (like skim milk) I would die for just about anybody. I want my skirt big and I want it to sweep. I want the camera to zoom in on my lips right before the pause, and I want my favourite poets at the animal ball. Richard Siken gets to dance with the zebra because he makes me cry the most. Anne Carson spikes the punch. She's got the quickest hands and there's 13 of her. We have our conversations in the shadows against red wallpaper, like:

–*I have a brick.*

–*Fact.*

–

–*I'm trying really hard to make it love.*

–

–*It already is.*
–*It already stopped.*

–

–*I am trying.*
–*So.*
–*Hard.*

Then switchblades fall from my ears and slit my collarbones. Everyone starts snapping and I tell them to shut up.

I ask the horse to strip and she starts sobbing because "It's Vera Wang", but that's not how the world works and I am the one with the switchblade.

It's such a funny story and the best part is no one ever remembers except for me, so I can tell it over

and over legs crossed, dress wide on the staircase, tapping my feet. Over,

and over, no one ever asks

for me to switch the scenes.

Over and over

I've written the whole play.

WE'LL MAKE A DEAL

I will watch the movie and you will read the book, because I've never seen the movie but I've read the book, and you've never read the book but you've seen the movie.

You will propose this. I will say, sounds fair to me.

I will say, good night. I will say, good bye.

I will look at you under the little light, head down in the driver's seat, plugging your address into your phone. You live 45 minutes away, so I'll wait 45 minutes, then I'll wait 20 more.

Then I'll watch the movie.

It will take 2 hours but the book will take you longer, so I'll go to the washroom and I'll grab a blanket, maybe a snack, and I'll play it from the start.

There will be a scene that I'll really want to talk to you about but I won't want to spoil the book for you, and I know you've seen the movie already but it's been a few years. So I'll wait.

I'll play it from the start.

How long is the book? I won't remember. I'll play it from the start.

Maybe you fall asleep, it happens, I'll just play it from the start.

I'll reach for my phone to ask you what page you're on but I'll grab the remote instead. I won't hear from you so I will play it from the start.

I won't hear from you.

I'll play it from the start.

I won't hear from you.

I'll play it from the start.

THE CHRISTIAN CYCLE / REDEMPTION / ETC

Let Eve kill herself.

   Naked and cowering—she wants to die for you.

   She wants to be her own.

   She is just a child and her hand is

sin. No one else can pluck that fruit.

      No one can speak to Adam.

         And now no one can speak to you.

   Let Eve kill herself or what of her daughters?

      Daughters aligned like beads on a horizontal

plane. Hearts skewered on the vertical

   axis of your judgment.

   What cycle?

Let there be

what?

FIGURA

there are quite a few poets who still operate in the figural,

figura, everything on earth a figure to be fulfilled,

a reference, the gesture to a beyond,

to wave one's heart at the sky like a dirty

washcloth—what are words for?

when I invoke you in my poem am I shooting the bird

to watch it land? am I shooting my own foot?

a gash of air from open streams. my grandfather passes

away. in the paper, nothing new.

up is no longer the only way.

the world opened long ago.

so you filled. right here you were filled.

but if that were true, why were you crying?

tell me,

why were you crying?

THE METRO

In Paris they call the subway Metro, here

the Metro is a stack of green newsprint at the

station, and if you arrive early enough

you can read along to the newscast overhead.

I don't have strong opinions on anything, other

than automatic flushing toilets, which are bad,

and, of course, bad things, which are also bad.

Nothing is well.

GOOD PASTA

Jonathan's Instagram is all photos of golf fields and Christmas lights.
He sweeps his hair back in a Bluejays cap and sings along to country songs.
I think about how easy it'd be to buy him presents. To make him happy.

I'd really like to make him happy.

The waitress calls him "Adam's brother" and offers us shots.

She says I can order any pasta and they'll make it, doesn't have to be on the menu.
I feel so special next to Adam's brother. I feel so lucky to be called into this scene.

I think it could be nice to leave my life behind, to be Adam's Brother's Girl.

I think it could be nice, so nice. I think I could be nice.

Jonathan drives home in the rain, I hope he gets back safe.
I hope he lives a happy life. I hope he thinks I'm nice.

INTERNET STALKER

some girls don't like other girls because they
make their living off boy-luv & we all know
there's not a lot of that to go around

HAVING A THURSDAY MORNING

Earlier I received an email from a friend, about a hypothetical future, about the past. I said:

something's in my eye! That is not true. There is sea brine in my lungs. That is also not true.

I do not know how to speak to my friends.

A blue jay appears in the yard and is scrubbed away. A red squirrel stays. Everything listens until the picture moves, and then we are on the train, all of us, all my friends.

There is always something in my eye. I just forgot. I must be late for something. I forget.

I have painted with a shaky hand. It's Thursday and already I am old.

PART 2

UNSOLICITED PORTRAITS

S.

I am sitting in the back of my friend's car,
trying not to make this a sad poem.
Are you sure you don't want to sit up front?
Have you ever been in love?

My friend takes me home, says I don't have to answer,
asks, *if your heart was a fruit what would it be?*

I love the highway at night, it's that simple,
it could be so simple. Someone honks their horn
and I go to open the door, to fight, then my friend
says her heart is an overripe peach
and I say *have you ever had a Saturn peach?*
Have you ever fought with teeth?

She's all teeth, teeth of a cherry tree,
she lets me play any song I want,
she lets me sing, she sings along.

I tell her I'm a yellow plum. I don't know what I am.
Somebody ate me. I ate myself.
Do I have a pit? Do you hold it in your mouth?
Can I be a tree?

The moon is gibbous and people are dancing on the street.
Sidewalk salsa, how romantic, how simple, how perfect.
I stand in my driveway, her car is white.

Wind blows through her rear-view
mirror. The branches of a tree,
dipped in water.

What I mean is,

They could.

H.

    In your other form you are a heron .

  freshwater coastal - grey , you wade

through cloud - reeds , stand on one leg to preserve

    heat . I ' m not sure you know the length

       of your wingspan . I ' m not sure you

    hear the hush that befalls .

Boy in freshwater , hair matted to forehead ,

   you cup your hands and form a lotus .

   Sapphire - lantern , rain on thatched roofs ,

      you breathe the mist that drifts the boat .

    Tomorrow ...   Tomorrow ...

      you ' re always the light

              Today and   again

           who sketches the dawn .

FOR MY SISTER

In which stories are peaches and grapes and we can look to a memory

without a pearl to crush. In which your mouth is full

of jam, mother is always home, and longing never reaches us.

> The sidewalk is a ruin of chalk, all our lines twisted into
> friendly shapes.

The neighbourhood is no longer new, you wake up early, there is no such thing.

Snow fills your bedroom masking all your dirty socks.

....

> On your dresser there's a book, in it a rabbit.
>
> I'll guard the hole and you grab
>
> > the stopwatch.
> >
> > > If you fall I'll lift you up.

M.

M cracks open an oyster with words:

> now there's a pearl
>
> now there's a movie

Twin to the moon, light over the highway / beaming red to red / to thread / a safety net

Pendant I, pendant you / side by side we make a charm / if you miss this flight you'll catch another / if you fall asleep you'll dream

Of ponds. Of minerals. / An audience / silenced / by you

Now there's a movie!

KIDS

1.

E and L were in the bathroom putting on eyeliner and I was asleep on the couch. I was trying to sleep. My birthday happened in the middle of the day. I was walking or in the back of a car. They wanted to look nice. L gave me her hoodie. I put my hands in the pockets and there was some stuff in there. I kept my mouth shut.

We took the streetcar. The girls shared vodka straight from the bottle. They offered me some and I said why would I want that it smells awful. L said yeah but it makes you feel good. I didn't think anything could. The street was loud and none of the girls wore coats. L took my hand and E led the way. Somebody pushed me. I was scared but mad too. I said who pushed me. I said who and L pulled me into the crowd. I didn't like letting things go. I'd have died in a grocery store brawl. It was my birthday. It wasn't my birthday but I told people it was because it always was. We went from one loud place to another and it was fine by me because I didn't have to talk.

E stopped talking to me because I did our entire project but I couldn't get a 90. Before we graduated she asked me for the stapler so I think we're cool. I gave L her hoodie back and she put her hands in the pockets. I looked away so she didn't have to say anything.

2.

my favourite memory of A: she's on the side of the road prying at her dog's mouth. it ate something it shouldn't have. a car pulled over and the window rolled down. her dog could have died. the driver threatened to call the cops. A walked up to the window and said fuck. fuck fuck fuck. fuck fuck fuck fuck fuck fuck fuck fuck. I wish I'd been there.

3.

We're cool? Yeah we're cool. Good I was worried you were mad at me. No we're cool. Cool.

PART 3

ARCADE

THERE CAME A GREAT BUZZ

What if you are full of mosquitoes?

What if a mosquito goes to suck your blood and she sucks and sucks and another mosquito comes out, and your mosquito says, "Oh. That's where you've been." and the other mosquito says, "There's nothing for you here."—what can the bear do with the honeycomb?

What if you put your ear to a seashell and it drowns you? I say, why can't it end with the wave? Why not? The lake is a great image. Under fog and grey light. Some end! When the sun set water covered my pupils, because we were by the shore, everything condensed. Behind my back there was a cackling, a fire, and one by one the mosquitoes flew out of me. There came a great crash. What if you were there? What if you knew?

What if you were just like me?

Could we open ourselves, maybe in the dark of a cave? Could you find a cave with your GPS? I am ashamed and my pain tolerance is not that high. Could a cave conceal my echo? It is dark in my stomach and there's no room to stretch my legs.

Here's what happens when you listen to the buzz in you.

Can you hear it?

The rain outside.

WINDSWEPT GAZER

7 months and still grieving the setting sun.

7 months and still looking back, watching you turn to stone.

Tableaux my faults and send them to me in a dream. Morning is an exit that eats itself.

Not wrong even when it's cruel. I place the backs of my hands on the table and you open the skylight. There's a scorpion in the center of solution. Where are the wells that catch my tears? Bringing them back to me in buckets. Where is the self that forgives?

Can I see her?

Can I have a horse? If I am to go

all this way, let me name a few things.

Forgive my not seeing.

There's a big oak tree in the field where you left me.

THIS POEM

Two different textures meet, one entering the other: a fluff drifting into jagged wood. A girl walks into the darkened wood and steps out a—still—a girl, wolfish. She is not young. She is young. It does not matter. One reality crosses with another, hashes, she is pressed against the crisscross she is: unshaped: lopped: repackaged or— broken out of? She is a girl. She is a boy. It does not matter. She is who she says she is she is lost, she is dripping, drilling, taking form: tossing it. Humming stretch the night in two. On, and on more: she is writing this poem.

KILL BILL: VOL. 1

Nancy Sinatra, the daughter not the wife, helps reimagine us in a desert town.

Either these places don't exist anymore or, bang bang, the world's grown larger.

I hit the ground—does a tumbleweed roll by at this moment or is that overkill?

If I die does that make me the hero? And what about Cher? It's her song.

Scenes are never filmed by temporal sequence.

Here you put a bullet in my head then we're getting coffee.

Then you're giving me a ride,

on your back, you lift me up. I'm asking you if I'm heavy:

am I heavy, am I heavy. How could I be?

Maybe we're the actors. We meet in the hotel lobby, bang bang,

let's grab coffee. Why is it always coffee?

I like to reimagine us as a Quentin Tarantino film because here the girls are

fighters, here their pain is sensationalized, here we watch

them suffer, watch them suffer, watch them suffer. Bang

bang. I don't have to re-imagine us. My baby shoots me down and somebody

makes a cover of it, and a cover of it, and a cover of it. What an awful sound.

1930S MICKEY MOUSE CLUB HOUSE MEETING

When I'm sad I feel like a packed theatre
of Mickey Mouse fans

When I'm sad everyone
wears a Mickey Mouse mask

When I'm sad it's 1930
A black and white photo

Not a spare seat in the crowd

A silent lobby

GOODFELLAS, 1990

"Business bad? Fuck you, pay me. Had a fire? Fuck you, pay me. The place got hit by lightning? Fuck you, pay me."

Janice had these great eyes. Like Liz Taylor's. Henry brings home the most expensive tree from the store. The massive white bulk of it barely fits through the door. Nobody tells him what to do. He opens his eyes into the barrel of a gun. Janice says it'll cost him but she looks good. A guy could get whacked just like that. When you're part of a crew nobody ever tells you when they're going to kill you. It's family. All he has to do is tell her he loves her a few times a year. Go shopping. Go buy yourself whatever you like. There's Dior dresses just around the corner. Go on. What's the matter with Janice. Why'd she have to go and get scared. They're just around that corner. This helicopter's been following me all day. I thought it was the cops but turns out it was god. I got nowhere else to go. You're all I got. And I really, really need your help.

SUSPIRIA

every day a different translation walks the streets

    one version of the self points back at another

I am supposed to look the same

                         something's off

I step out of myself to look at myself

and oh

and oh

I am

so sorry

                    6 million mes walk

            through and through each other

                air laced with reflection

something's off

                        pushing

                  forward going

                      onward

something's off

                something's free

something's lost

YOUR RIGHT EYE IS LAZY, THE LEFT EYE DOES ALL THE WORK

My foot made an imprint
on the carpet that looked like three
distinct animals.

In the order they appeared—
although having been there all along—a
tiger, a scorpion, and a leopard. I won't
describe their orientation to you.

The scorpion head stretches.
Coughing sounds from the room
down the hall. Everywhere is carpet
but the padding is wearing out.
You would need to strip the whole
house down to dust.

Growing up I was afraid to play
with marbles, afraid to swallow them.
My own hands can betray me. Awake in my
stranger's head. *Who's voice is calling
me to dinner* and will I go?
Will I go
together?

PSYCHO

Someone pours chocolate milk in the shower

and it mingles with the water swirling

down the drain. The camera catches blood.

There's a camera in the shower. Didn't they

tell you? Didn't they tell you this was a trick?

Say! Where on this grey hill did you park that car?

And do you hear birds? There's always some figure

in some rear-window! I won't tell you how it ends.

OPEN SCENE

A scene is taking place in the little coffee shop on Spadina. Tables and stools have been pushed to the center of the floor in a haste. The rest of the place is still under construction. Two actors share one script. There is no room to sit on the same side of the table so one is always reading their lines upside down, or not reading at all, staring out the window-walls, waiting their turn.

Outside, the tires are being pried off someone's bike. One actor interrupts the other to ask if the bike belongs to them. The other actor shakes their head no. They continue to read. Then one of the actors notices that the lines are written in Latin. Luckily, there is a drop-in seminar on Latin. That actor leaves. Once outside, they realize that the bike is theirs. They return defeated only to find the coffee shop full. They manage to find a seat near the back. Someone passes them a bucket of popcorn. The actor asks for more butter but their request is denied. They see that they have been replaced by the barista, who knows even less Latin than they do.

Two actors lock eyes. One of them walks warily up to the podium. People step forward holding up garlands, which touch the actor's head. Words come up-side down.

BUZZFEED PREDICTS MY BREAKUP

The figure emerges through the library door and scoffs when he sees me reading a sci-fi paperback. Or maybe he scoffs at my skirt. Or maybe he has phlegm in his throat.

He takes his shirt from me and asks for the time. He swears. He says see you later.

It's a slip, but it annoys me. I can't put my book away fast enough to run after him, to say, no. I will never see you again. You will die and I will die and we will never see each other again.

A few weeks later he will send me his novel manuscript. He's so @GuyInYourMFA. I will say, "Your character never learns from his mistakes." He will say, "I thought it was a happy ending." I will say, "It's not a real ending." He will say, "Okay."

I will think about the part I played in preventing the next Woody Allen. Or failing to prevent.

Buzzfeed says I will reunite with my tenth-grade crush. I want to know the calamities.

PART 4

BLUE OLIVES

PLAINWATER

like blue olives from the sky. these round shapes that come a-prattle on the night. you text me about the rain from the floor of your truck. your radio tick-tacking the whole drive home. my vocal chords swell. this night like round things inside me. I had no idea.

FRIEND

Someone passes by the window who looks like you.
He has his head down, reading from his phone.
I wonder if you got my message.

ON ANNE CARSON

A morning so cold that, walking up the hairpin

that marks the end of my neighbourhood, I do not

stop to pet the neighbour's dog. Sweet dog, the poodle.

Beauty makes Carson hopeless and it makes me

hopeless. I have her in my bag, anyway, for the trip.

Train-dreams are general and often cut short. Not

often but always. Not cut but hung like a bird's

cry, jewels on air. Someone has taken my spot in

the coach. It does not occur to me to reach over and

spread my madness over everything, or that it is an

idealized form of madness, that it leaves room

for wisdom and humanity. There are other seats to take.

Look. Carson cuts and cuts deep to find the source of the

problem. She parts her heart to either side like hair.

Hopeless to gather what falls. Do you dream of her too.

ALLERGENS

Cherry drain, we hue ourselves into the think-tank

bottom of the wine glass, sunday again.
I suck the outer corners of my mouth,
drawing in my cheeks: all the bodies
                      waiting to be formed with words.

My body waiting to be deconstructed

sitting through spring then bubbling some.
I want to bring you a gift.
I want to bring you a gift.
    I want to bring you a gift.

These hands won't do
anymore.

NINE WHISPER-SHELLS

I am standing on a plain. It is a light
    feeling. The grass is yellow and I
        am thinking about my favourite book.
There's a circle somewhere. Which is to say
    I am young
again.
I see a seaside village that is not in the tale.
        A map of Ancient Greece is projected
            over its streets,
    only the cat is real.
The world is run down and blue for miles. Which is to say I am the
    oldest person by light
speed.
    Which is to say, only the cat.
At the eleventh hour I will go down to the village and
        try not to step on the conch
            (*con-scious con-scious*)

shells. I mark the ones I've already listened to with

    dry berries. Even the cat doesn't know

        about the memories.

I pick a shell and press it against my chest. I move it to

the left.

    Which is to say, I am looking,

            for you.

SOME TREES

Some trees remind me of other

trees. I could never get their colours quite

right with acrylics. But make a field

and we could lay in it. A field at last, each step a crush

of lavender. When I speak I beetle-tongue. I tuck

my knees to my chest and hide my jaw. There are still

many flowers I haven't learned to name.

I bring them to you: my arms

full

of silence.

ANOTHER TRY

thoughts

turn into pointed stars

whisker prick

can't spend my whole life

monitoring me

weight of fog in my ear canal

cream on skin soothe   my summer

    sneeze

        caked sleeper

    slow cooked

all I want is every night

all I want is

        furry feeling

        head high

    all I want   to risk

IMAGINE

wet sky against eye,

snow warm dripping.

there's a roof we could

be on. night blur pattern

broke my leg in a dream.

imagine being slip-proof.

shingle for heart-hold,

something needs repairing.

weight sunk. weight

sinking imagine breathing.

boat-bodies not jumping.

the waves dance.

IT'S TRUE

Friend,

I bought new stationery. Forty dollars for some paper and envelopes and now I have

Nothing to search for

I think

I'd like to live in a place with swallows. I think that's where I grew up

Every morning the same two swallows fan the air. Although my mother hasn't read me that poem since I was a kid. Last year she was sick

This year she isn't

If I don't shampoo after the pool my hair squeezes itself wave-like

Strand-strand the prettiest I've looked in weeks. I watch girls tan

On a cloudy day. Upgrade the blender and fill it with ice

My boyfriend buys a fake grass carpet for his balcony. At first I laugh but then

I sit

We have all our meals here. Fish tacos and Pina Coladas, pineapple chicken quinoa salad. Everything is made

From scratch

Beer foams on a green grid. The pool spills

Off the seventh floor

I can't face   simple living

UR BEDROOM AT 4AM

is not quite orange.

not sure how to reach u

now that ur angry.

I see a crow's tongue.

I don't like it. the sky,

the clearing, who knew

it would be this blue.

I see through ur window

at me in ur bed

just sitting, seeing the same.

see: I'm almost up to me.

it's almost clearing.

see: how bad I am at lying.

BOY

BOY has his own condo and I love to play house. BOY kisses my eye with his wet beer mouth. I nearly blinded myself trying to put on makeup. BOY says I can shower then BOY gets in with me. The water is hot and there's no air. How can I sing?

                                      How can I sing?

CHAMOMILE TEA

hidden away in anime rain,

it's early afternoon. the world makes a lot of sense.

for lavender light takes the window and even

      shock can soothe. I wait around for the harm.

      powder white, soft on skin,

           winter morning marigold night.

    rain—but someone drew this.

    rain—someone's desire.

it feels as if I can't get lost.   can pastel be kind?

    can a colour tell me where to go?

    is the moon filled with bells?

will the frames slip themselves, drip and pool the time?

avalanche of petal thoughts

    a touch of   pink perhaps a touch   of you.

PART 5

CONCERT

FOR MY FRIENDS, WHO SAVE ME

GRAND, I am grand. I am two   birds

stacked. One by one. I am a friend.

    A tower of sparrows, dirty and simple.

There's nowhere to be   no rush. I make a bonfire

with a poem. I gather leaves and make a roof. I watch

    you. One by one. Here come my friends.

Chirping in a rainbow floating on a puddle. Easy.

I'm clutched in a claw. Easy.

    The shadow of a hawk.   Easy.

Dirty and simple, one one one, we stack ourselves

        and stack some more.

STADIUM SHOW

I can see the shimmering surface / almond milk in all the trees / and nobody's face.

There's a concert tomorrow night in the baseball stadium downtown.
I have a ticket for the last row, behind a few thousand people. It will feel

primal. All the different kinds of being alive.

Say: you call me at night / raw throat.   Say: I press my slick palm against yours.

Say winter.   Say fall.

Sun sting moon pain drizzy hilltop blue.

Can you feel it?

Train shaking / nothing spilling.
My cheek on the window   and nobody's hand.

Say I text you.

Say you text me back.

A few thousand people / singing along.

GUIDE

Today, I am tempted

to polish the hardwood,

study the genus and name

of every tree in Ontario,

plug my phone in and lay

it on the nightstand when

my eyes are too tired to read.

      Searching for beauty

          in my own mind,

trying to put it there.

Tossing on a twin bed

until all my promises break.

Crowded by the past of it.

And from what I've seen

You can tell that the water is going

down by the silt on the leaves.

You can boil water in the pad of

a prickly pear. To smoke a rattlesnake,

wind the meat around the arms

of a young branch.

There is a simple direction to

everything.

SURPRISE GIFT

Mad luck—when you sunk

backs of hands in the growth and dug

up something fresh. What potato here?

Hearth and home and breath, on a window,

light out. Drawn out—and rewarded so!

Handsome this grey day. Handsome

your calloused hands. Now is the time

to cry, if you wish, if you have ever

wanted to weep. Do it now over the sink

with the warm water gushing.

Such the surprise of gifts.

ALL THE THINGS YOU HAVE ARE REAL

I had my head down in my sister's

room when I heard the first splash.

I ran to a different window but I couldn't

see my dad outside. I ran downstairs

and found him in the kitchen. The whole sky

slamming on the deck. You got caught

in the rain, I say. It just came down.

I heard a splash then it just came down.

All at once like an upturned bucket.

After I say this I go back upstairs,

where it is warm.

CROSS COUNTRY

Who can sleep?

The sun makes the ice look a certain gold.

Someone made a circle over the water, I wonder what they saw.

Another world beneath this one?

Water tundra. Snow tundra.

Ice so bright under my eyelids.

So sharp a morning and it's only Friday.

The train sings.

I had thought I missed the good things.

I had thought they weren't for me.

THIS YEAR

maybe you press a letter against the window and try to make out the words, maybe the light pushes through the page into your eye, white rainbow, maybe you draw a brilliant arc with the branch by your feet, maybe your shoes are worn out but maybe you don't remember walking in them, maybe you sell flowers on a snowy day, maybe a stranger kisses your cheek, maybe you want something, maybe you have something that's not yours, maybe you're holding your breath, maybe you blow out all the candles in one try, maybe every year it gets harder, maybe every year it gets brighter, maybe the letter isn't addressed to anyone and maybe it isn't sealed, maybe you read it and maybe you set it down, maybe this. maybe *this* is the year

ENDLESS SUMMER (TOPS LIVE SCORE)

Summer begins with salt

Water

    Waves and

A bump near your eyebrow,

                Raised,

  Dancing on water

Two steps forward

Two steps back

Squatting, arms out, skimming

 A familiar stranger singing

    Outside, you don't know why

        You enter

        It's yellow

        The perfect wave

How much of surfing is just

Falling off and getting

Back on?

How much of the dream

Is reimagined

By summer?

How much of summer

Is dreamed?

Pulled by the flute

Carriage

Carried   Carried

FLASH STORM

I can admit the truth now that it is quiet and you are with me.

    Cozy in separate rooms, lightning entering through our respective windowpanes.

        Look at the light on the glass, the wave over your head, your music.

            There isn't a part of it that isn't cruel.

                My favourite poets are dying, Crush, your flickering image.

                    Crush, I beat the heat. I only write you.

                      Underneath a branch taking up somebody else's space. Obsessed with apologizing.

                        I am with indeterminable dread—

                          such a fancy way of saying I'm afraid.

                            Such a way to say that the moon is a mirror

to the sun, a door for dancing and a door for wasting time.

            Maybe a mouth isn't much, maybe everyone's talking.

                    Maybe the night can still be a mystery.

PATCHES

Belly skimming water, such a
bird thing, buggy boys in a flock
sundancing. We all have homes
to build in the dusk.

Thistle in the wheels of a bike,
a crawling tree. Take nothing
but a broken back, distance
growing yellow in patches,
patches, last night escapes
out a barn window.

Sweetness in the air. Two bowls
of corn water each. How *right*
to be umbrella'd. Warm enough
to unfold.

PERENNIAL

Morning rows its little boat, fluttering

curtains, my other self left

her white journal open

on the table for me to find

six am, I put sound in both my ears,

as if a wound was unwound,

unwound the clock, how did snow

there's no mistaking a tulip

planted before hard frost

turning the volume in spring

little handheld radio, water

GREEN

Ice ladder in the dirt

with coral. Sea chrysanthemum.

A compass with North four

times, pointing to them all at once.

There is nothing in particular

growing from my forehead

except that I haven't eaten in three

days. I'm not hungry and I don't

have the money.

Acid rain can turn this garden

rose.

Not being pulled.

Being pulled.

Shattered rainbow set

aflame when sound is not available, in

my country. Country of dogs, meaning

circle, meaning wolf, meaning wet

vulture over golden fields.

The lake has elbows, sweet

crook, find the joints.

Might that you say broken, might you make the call. Droplet on a green stalk—going up?

See where I tried to build something without a mirror: I am at infinity: still bounce.

To whom must I apologize?

My throat is infinite,

I accept myself.

Green and

going already.

ACKNOWLEGEMENTS

I want to express my gratitude to the dear editors of the following publications who published some of the poems in this book:

"Internet Stalker" appeared in *Metatron Press.*

"Kill Bill Vol. 1" appeared in *Peach Mag* Season 3.

"Kids" appeared in *Soft Cartel.*

"1930s Mickey Mouse Club House Meeting" appeared in *BAD DOG.*

"chamomile tea" appeared in *The Trinity Review* 131: Spring.

"For my friends, who save me" appeared in *The Puritan.*

"Surprise Gift" appeared in *Hart House Review.*

To my publishers and to Jim for directing me. E for the art. H for the walks. A for the tarot readings. N for socks. And to Y, which stands for You, of course it's you, always, thank you.

ABOUT THE AUTHOR

Lily Wang is the founding editor of *Half a Grapefruit Magazine*. She is doing her MA in English and Creative Writing at the University of Toronto. Her first chapbook *Everyone In Your Dream is You* was published by Anstruther Press in 2018. Her work has appeared in *Peach Mag, The Puritan, The Hart House Review, Bad Nudes, Hobart Pulp*, and more.